101 Daily Challenges

A Road Map for Teens

Megan Egerton
&
John Willman

Please Read

The authors have done their best to present accurate and up-to-date information in this book, but they cannot guarantee that the information is correct or will suit your particular situation. This book is sold with the understanding that the publisher and authors are not engaged in rendering legal, accounting, counselling or any other professional services. If expert assistance is required, the services of a competent professional should be sought.

Copyright 2011 Egerton Graham Consulting
ISBN 9780981143668
Version 1.1

Author: Megan Egerton Graham

Design and Illustration: John Willman

Published by Egerton Graham Consulting
www.egertongrahamconsulting.com

www.WhileYouWereAway.Org

For Maya & Ethan,

Who challenge us every day!

Forward

Being a teen isn't easy at the best of times. In this book there are 101 challenges to make you think, teach you about yourself and the world around you. Have fun with them and take the time you need to learn from each challenge and experience.
Good Luck!

Tell
someone
something
you admire
about them

Date Completed:

What happened?

What did you learn about yourself?

Date Completed: _____

What happened?

_____
_____
_____
_____
_____

What did you learn about yourself?

_____
_____
_____
_____
_____
_____
_____

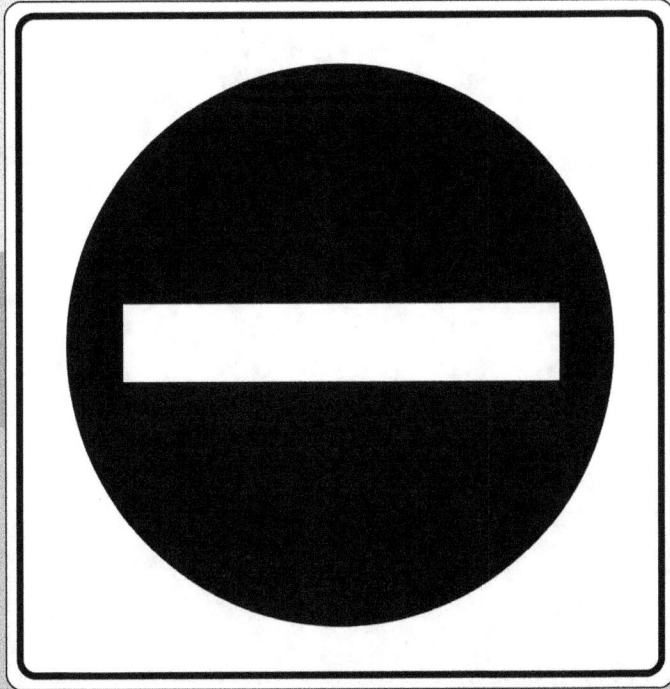

Introduce yourself to someone you don't know and ask them about themselves

Sit With Different People in Your Class

Date Completed:

What happened?

What did you learn about yourself?

Date Completed: _____

_____

What happened?

_____
_____
_____
_____
_____

What did you learn about yourself?

_____
_____
_____
_____
_____
_____
_____
_____

Date Completed:

What happened?

What did you learn about yourself?

NORTH
62

Tell a family
member
why
they are
important to
you

Listen to someone else's problems without offering a solution

Date Completed:

What happened?

What did you learn about yourself?

Date Completed:

What happened?

What did you learn about yourself?

Take an hour out of your day to do something for someone else for FREE

Date Completed: _____

_____

What happened?

_____

_____

_____

_____

_____

What did you learn about yourself?

_____

_____

_____

_____

_____

_____

_____

_____

_____

_____

_____

Date Completed: _____

What happened?

_____
_____
_____
_____
_____
_____

What did you learn about yourself?

_____
_____
_____
_____
_____
_____
_____
_____

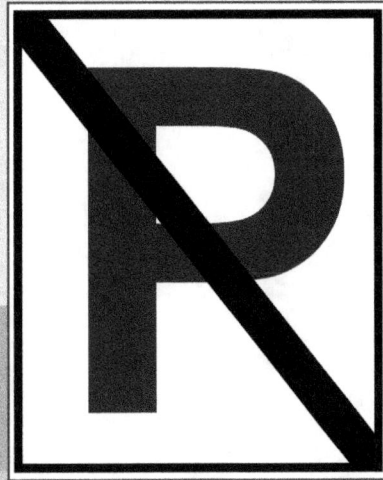

Tell a teacher what you like most about their class or teaching style

Date Completed:

What happened?

What did you learn about yourself?

NORTH
62

Look at yourself in the mirror and name 5 things you like about yourself

Date Completed: _____

_____

What happened? _____

_____

_____

_____

_____

_____

What did you learn about yourself?

_____

_____

_____

_____

_____

_____

_____

_____

Tell someone about a fear you have

Date Completed:

What happened?

What did you learn about yourself?

Decide on 5 things you would like to do before finishing school

Date Completed:

What happened?

What did you learn about yourself?

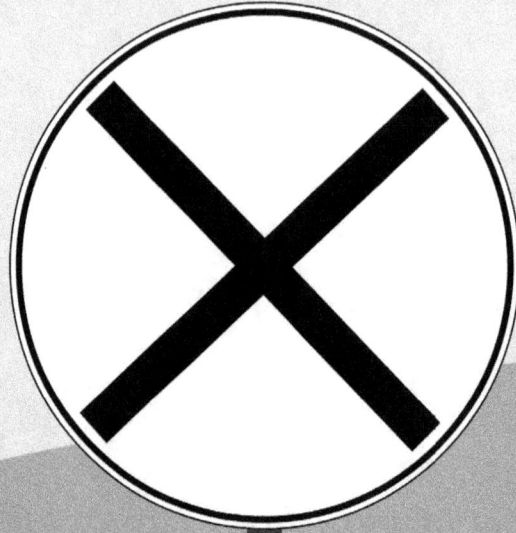

Tell someone
about a dream
or goal you have
and why you
have it

Date Completed:

What happened?

What did you learn about yourself?

Date Completed: _____

_____

What happened? _____

_____

_____

_____

_____

_____

_____

What did you learn about yourself?

_____

_____

_____

_____

_____

_____

_____

_____

Share
your most
embarrassing
moment

Paint a picture

Date Completed:

What happened?

What did you learn about yourself?

Ask
someone
in your family
what you can do
to make their day
easier

Date Completed: _____

What happened?
_____
_____
_____
_____
_____
_____

What did you learn about yourself?
_____
_____
_____
_____
_____
_____
_____
_____
_____
_____
_____

Date Completed:

What happened?

What did you learn about yourself?

Make a plan to go to the movies and include as many people as you can

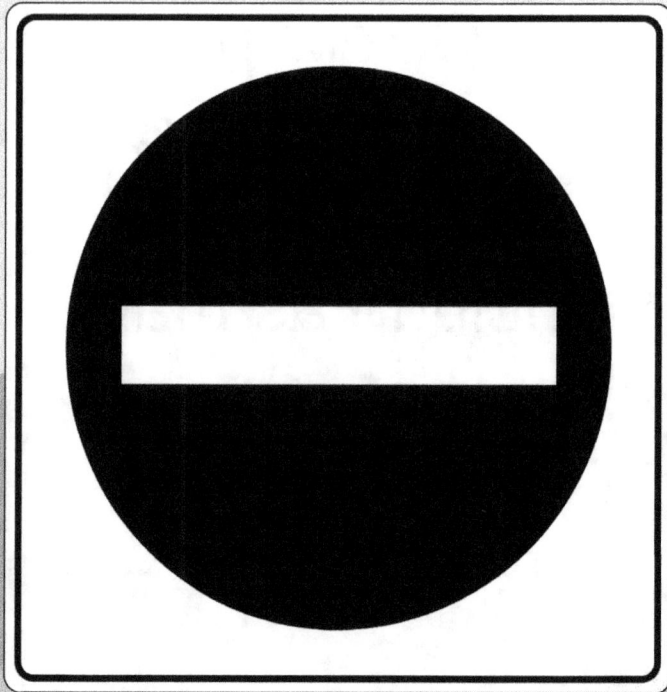

Organize your
locker or room
without being
asked to

Date Completed:

What happened?

What did you learn about yourself?

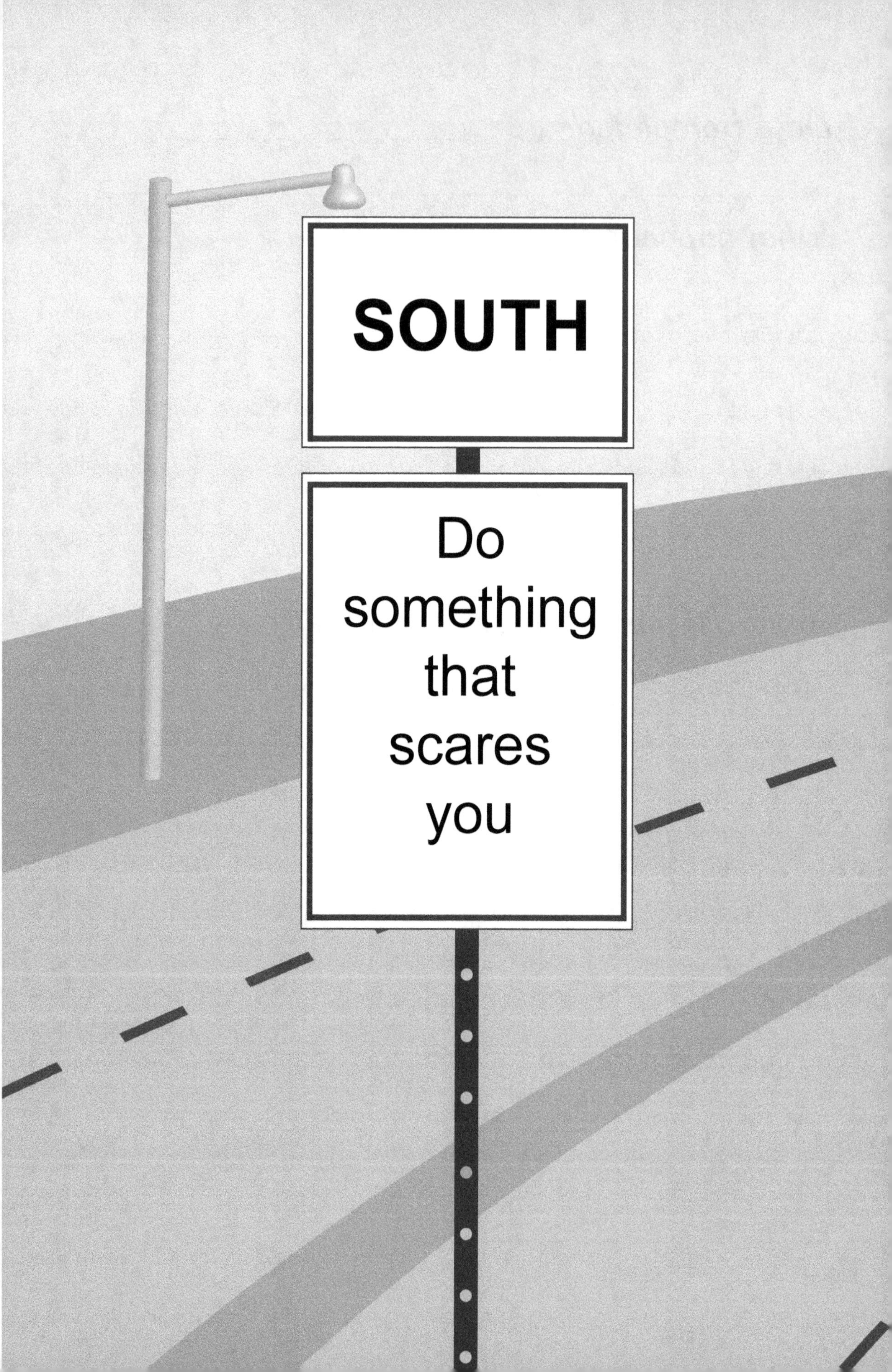
SOUTH
Do something that scares you

Date Completed:

What happened?

What did you learn about yourself?

Do something unpredictable or out of character

Date Completed:

What happened?

What did you learn about yourself?

Tell someone about the best vacation you ever had

GO WEST

Date Completed: _____

_____

What happened?
_____

_____

_____

_____

_____

_____

What did you learn about yourself?
_____

_____

_____

_____

_____

_____

_____

_____

_____

_____

_____

Go

Eat something
you never
have before

Date Completed: _____

What happened?

_____

_____

_____

_____

_____

_____

What did you learn about yourself?

_____

_____

_____

_____

_____

_____

_____

_____

_____

_____

_____

Try a sport you haven't ever tried before

Date Completed: _____

_____

What happened?

_____

_____

_____

_____

_____

What did you learn about yourself?

_____

_____

_____

_____

_____

_____

_____

_____

_____

Date Completed:

What happened?

What did you learn about yourself?

Say positive things all day

GO

Tackle a problem
you have been
avoiding

Date Completed:

What happened?

What did you learn about yourself?

CALL

Call a relative or friend you haven't seen in awhile

Date Completed: _____

_____

What happened?

_____

_____

_____

_____

_____

What did you learn about yourself?

_____

_____

_____

_____

_____

_____

_____

_____

_____

_____

_____

Date Completed:

What happened?

What did you learn about yourself?

Tell someone you love them

(that you normally take for granted)

Do something for the environment

Date Completed:

What happened?

What did you learn about yourself?

Date Completed:

What happened?

What did you learn about yourself?

Date Completed: _____

_____

What happened?

_____

_____

_____

_____

_____

_____

What did you learn about yourself?

_____

_____

_____

_____

_____

_____

_____

_____

Do something that is just for...

you

Listen to music...

your parents like

Date Completed: _____

_____

What happened?

_____

_____

_____

_____

What did you learn about yourself?

_____

_____

_____

_____

_____

_____

_____

_____

Date Completed: _____

What happened? _____
_____
_____
_____
_____

What did you learn about yourself?
_____
_____
_____
_____
_____
_____
_____
_____

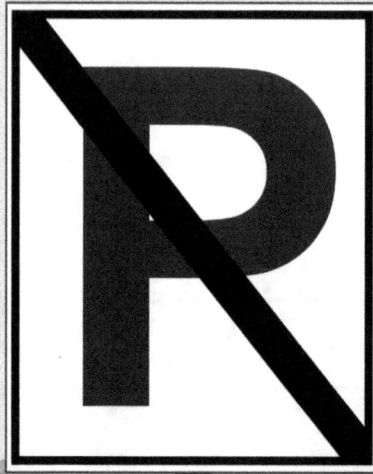

Date Completed:

What happened?

What did you learn about yourself?

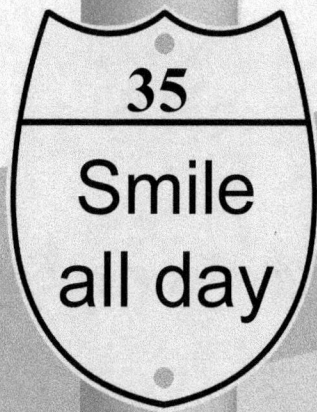

35

Smile
all day

Date Completed:

What happened?

What did you learn about yourself?

Date Completed:

What happened?

What did you learn about yourself?

Tell someone
why they are
important to
you...

in a
letter
or
email

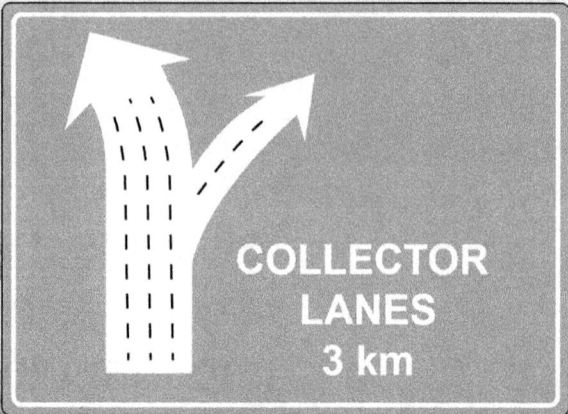

Date Completed:

What happened?

What did you learn about yourself?

Do something
you don't want
to do

Date Completed: _____

What happened?

_____

_____

_____

_____

_____

What did you learn about yourself?

_____

_____

_____

_____

_____

_____

_____

_____

_____

_____

Date Completed: _____

_____

What happened?

_____

_____

_____

_____

_____

What did you learn about yourself?

_____

_____

_____

_____

_____

_____

_____

_____

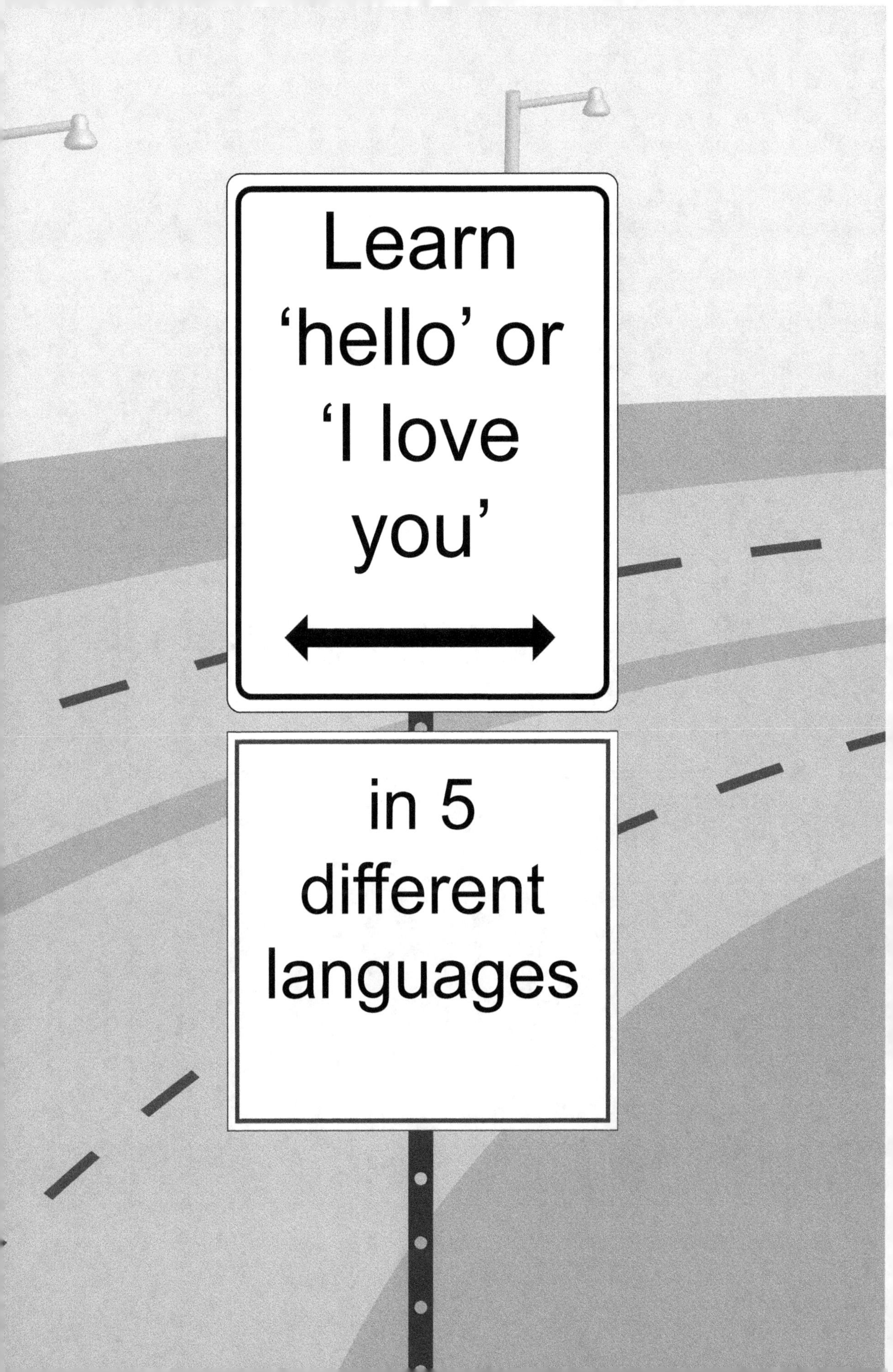
Learn
‘hello’ or
‘I love
you’
in 5
different
languages

3 Go for a hike

Date Completed:

What happened?

What did you learn about yourself?

Date Completed:

What happened?

What did you learn about yourself?

Read
a
book

P

Make a
'to do'
list for
your life

→

Date Completed: _____

What happened? _____

_____

_____

_____

_____

_____

What did you learn about yourself? _____

_____

_____

_____

_____

_____

_____

_____

_____

Date Completed: _____

_____

What happened?

_____

_____

_____

_____

_____

_____

What did you learn about yourself?

_____

_____

_____

_____

_____

_____

_____

_____

Go
and see a
movie you don't
think you are
interested
in

Write an editorial...

to your local newspaper

Date Completed:

What happened?

What did you learn about yourself?

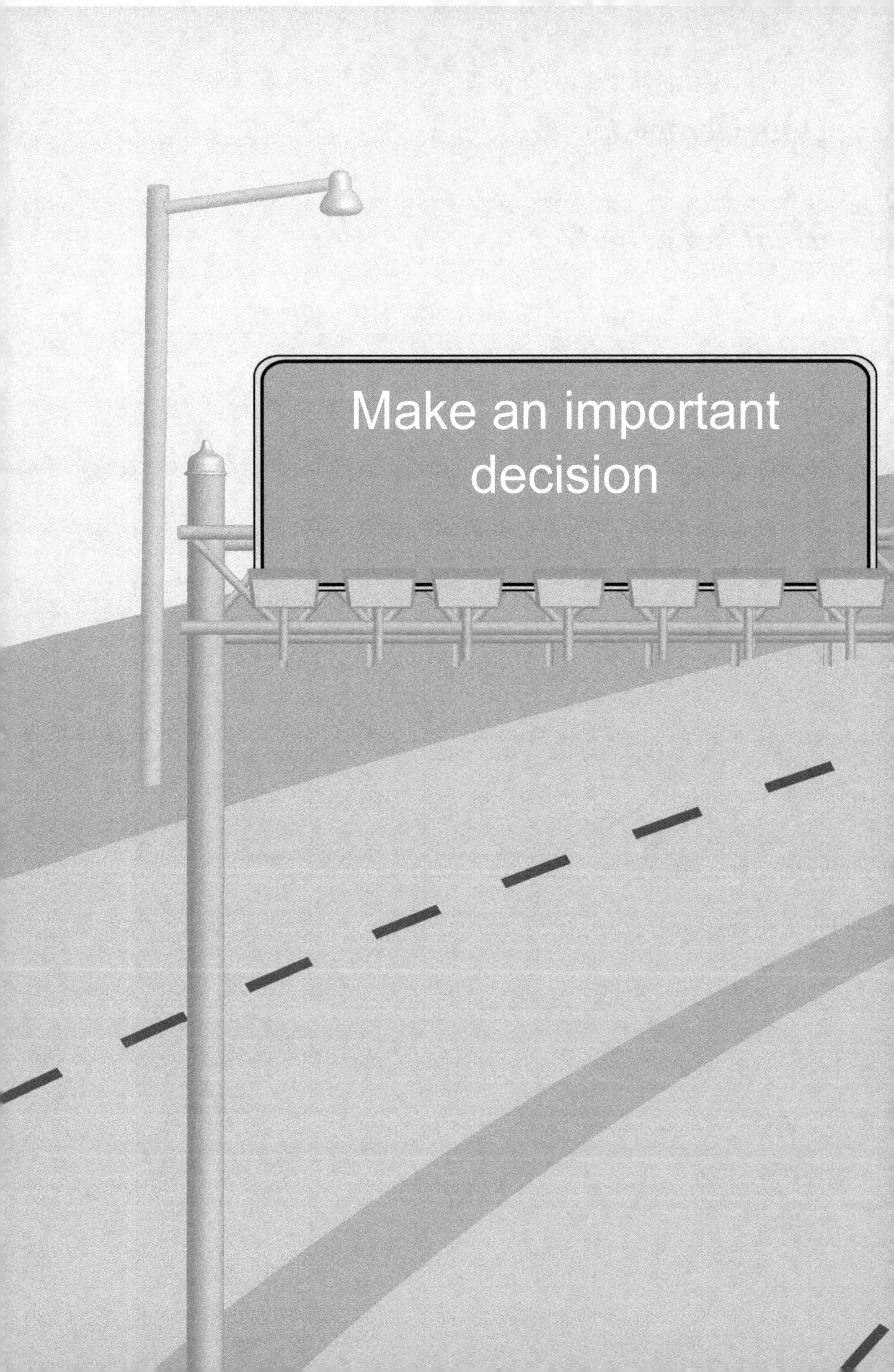
Make an important
decision

Date Completed:

What happened?

What did you learn about yourself?

Forgive someone

Date Completed:

_____

What happened?

_____

_____

_____

_____

_____

What did you learn about yourself?

_____

_____

_____

_____

_____

_____

_____

_____

_____

_____

Date Completed: _____

_____

What happened?

_____
_____
_____
_____
_____
_____

What did you learn about yourself?

_____
_____
_____
_____
_____
_____
_____
_____
_____

Don't swear

for the entire day

Wash a car
for someone
else

Date Completed:

What happened?

What did you learn about yourself?

Ask a
teacher
for help

Date Completed: _____

_____

What happened?

_____

_____

_____

_____

_____

_____

What did you learn about yourself?

_____

_____

_____

_____

_____

_____

_____

_____

_____

_____

Date Completed:

What happened?

What did you learn about yourself?

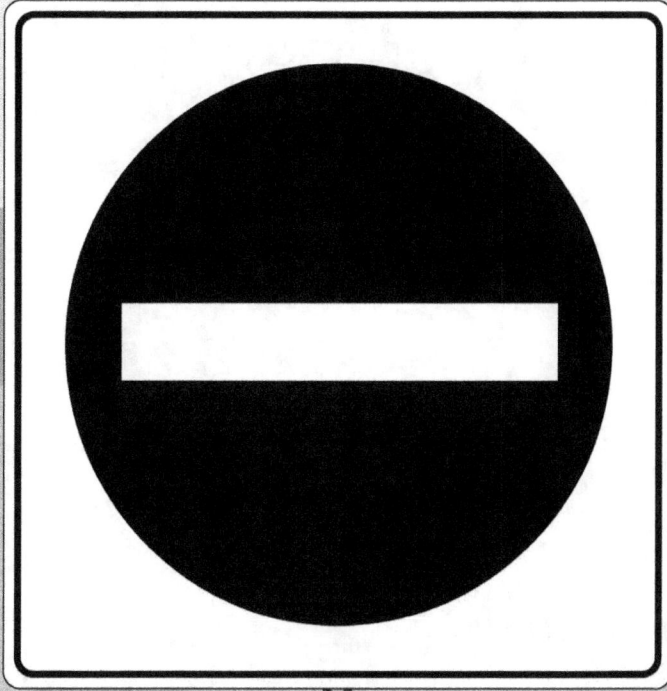

Paint

a

room

Make cookies or muffins and share them with as many different people as possible

Date Completed:

What happened?

What did you learn about yourself?

Date Completed:

What happened?

What did you learn about yourself?

Ask your parent for help

Date Completed: _____

What happened? _____

_____

_____

_____

_____

_____

What did you learn about yourself?

_____

_____

_____

_____

_____

_____

_____

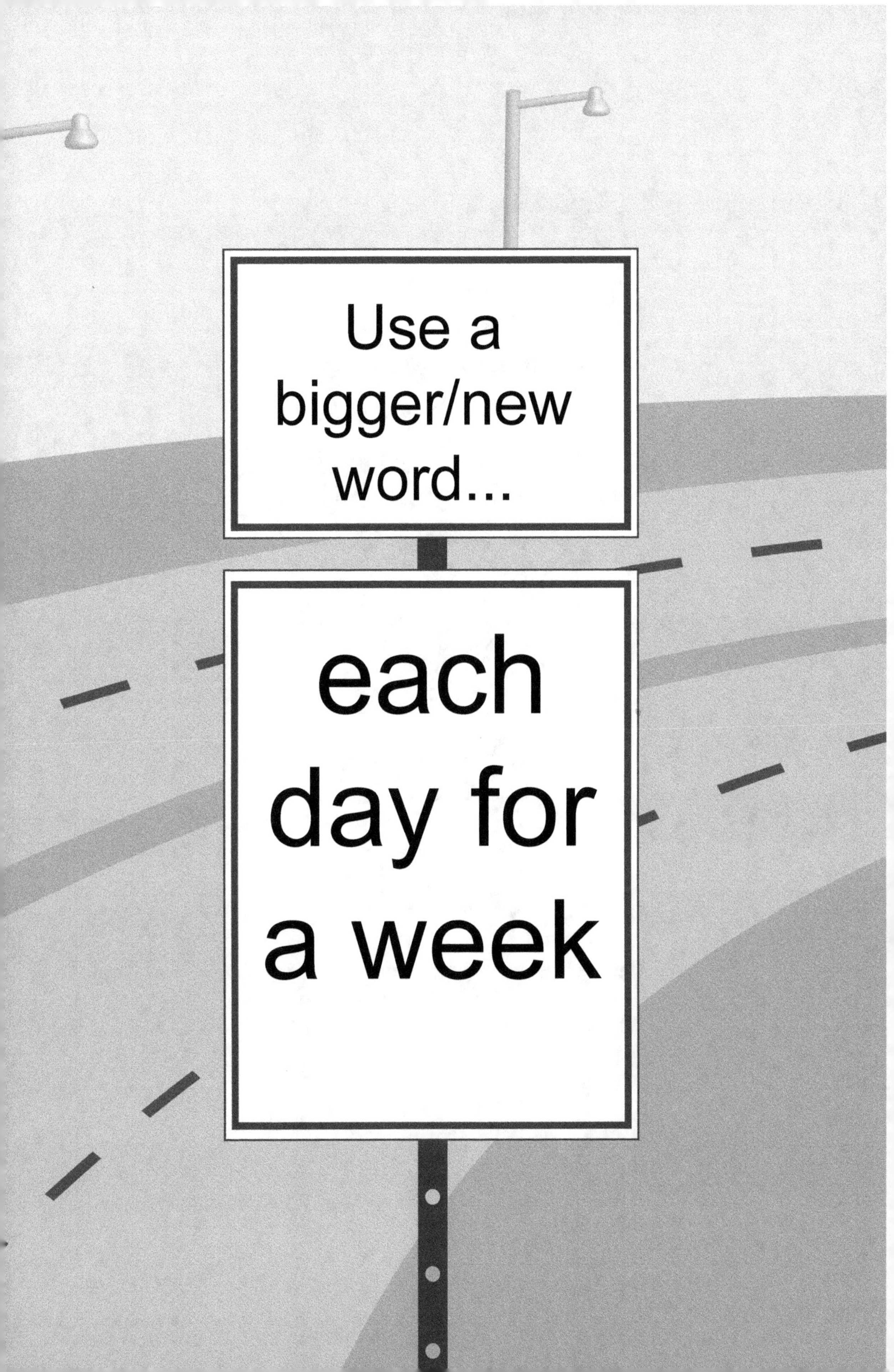
Use a bigger/new word...
each day for a week

Date Completed:

What happened?

What did you learn about yourself?

Date Completed:

What happened?

What did you learn about yourself?

Give someone a hug when they really need it

Date Completed: _____

What happened? _____

_____

_____

_____

_____

_____

What did you learn about yourself? _____

_____

_____

_____

_____

_____

_____

_____

_____

Date Completed: _____

_____

What happened?

_____

_____

_____

_____

_____

_____

What did you learn about yourself?

_____

_____

_____

_____

_____

_____

_____

_____

_____

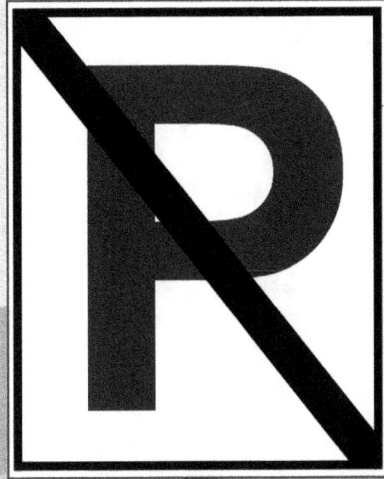

Date Completed: _____

_____

What happened?

_____

_____

_____

_____

_____

What did you learn about yourself?

_____

_____

_____

_____

_____

_____

_____

_____

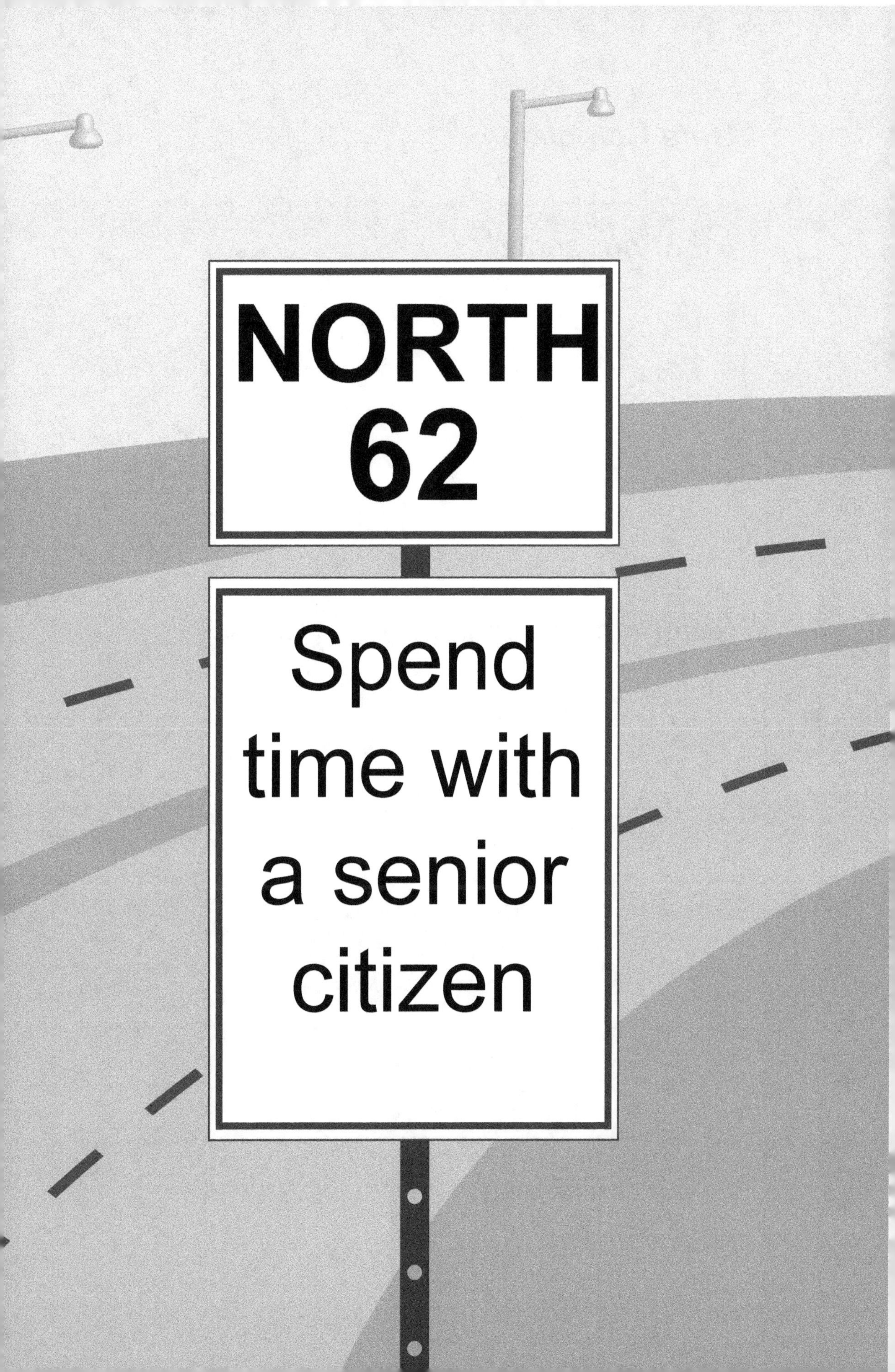
NORTH
62
Spend
time with
a senior
citizen

Date Completed: _____

_____

What happened?

_____
_____
_____
_____
_____
_____

What did you learn about yourself?

_____
_____
_____
_____
_____
_____
_____
_____
_____

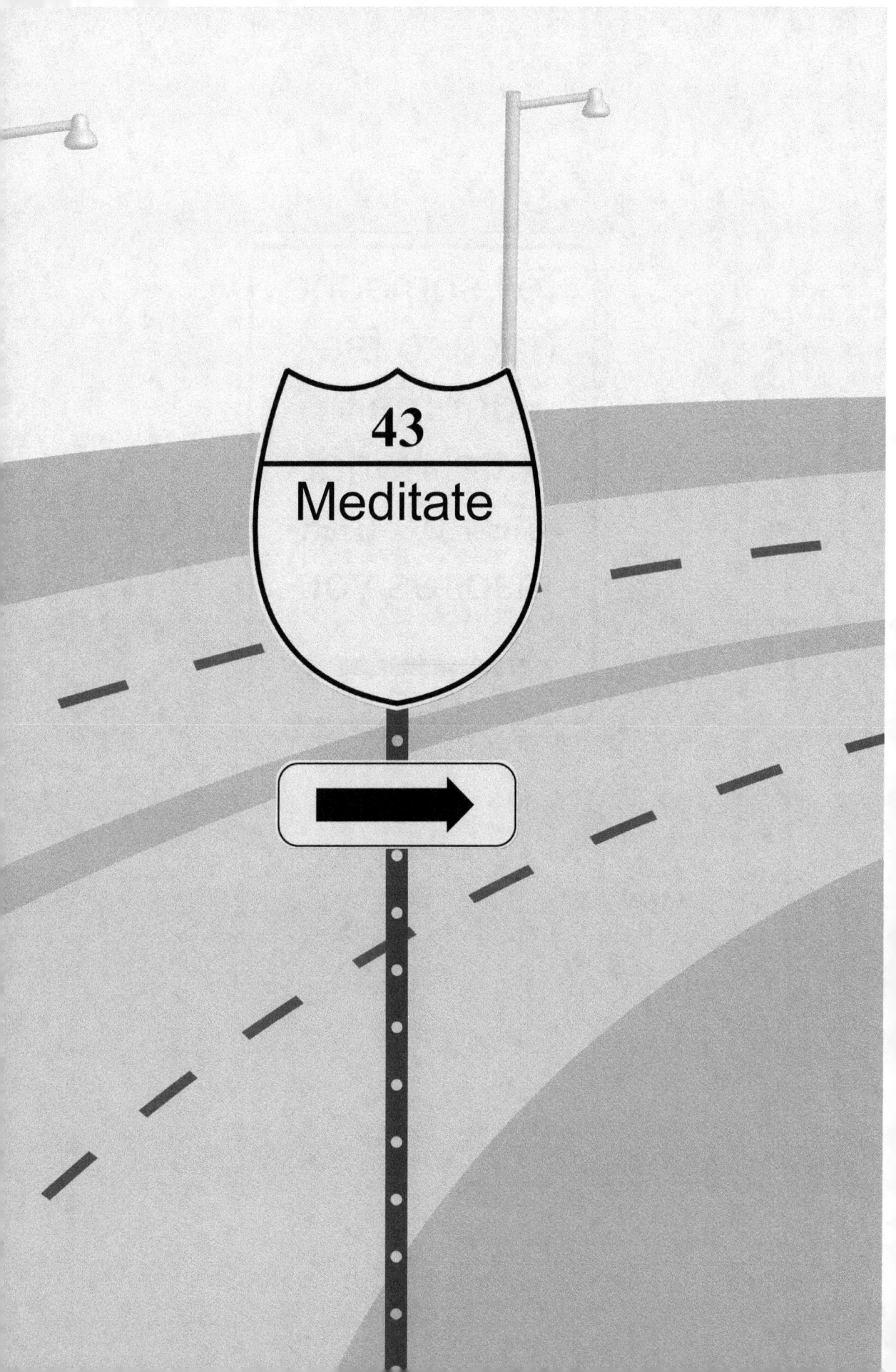

Tell someone
(face to face
or email/
letter) what
they do that
inspires you

⟷

Date Completed:

What happened?

What did you learn about yourself?

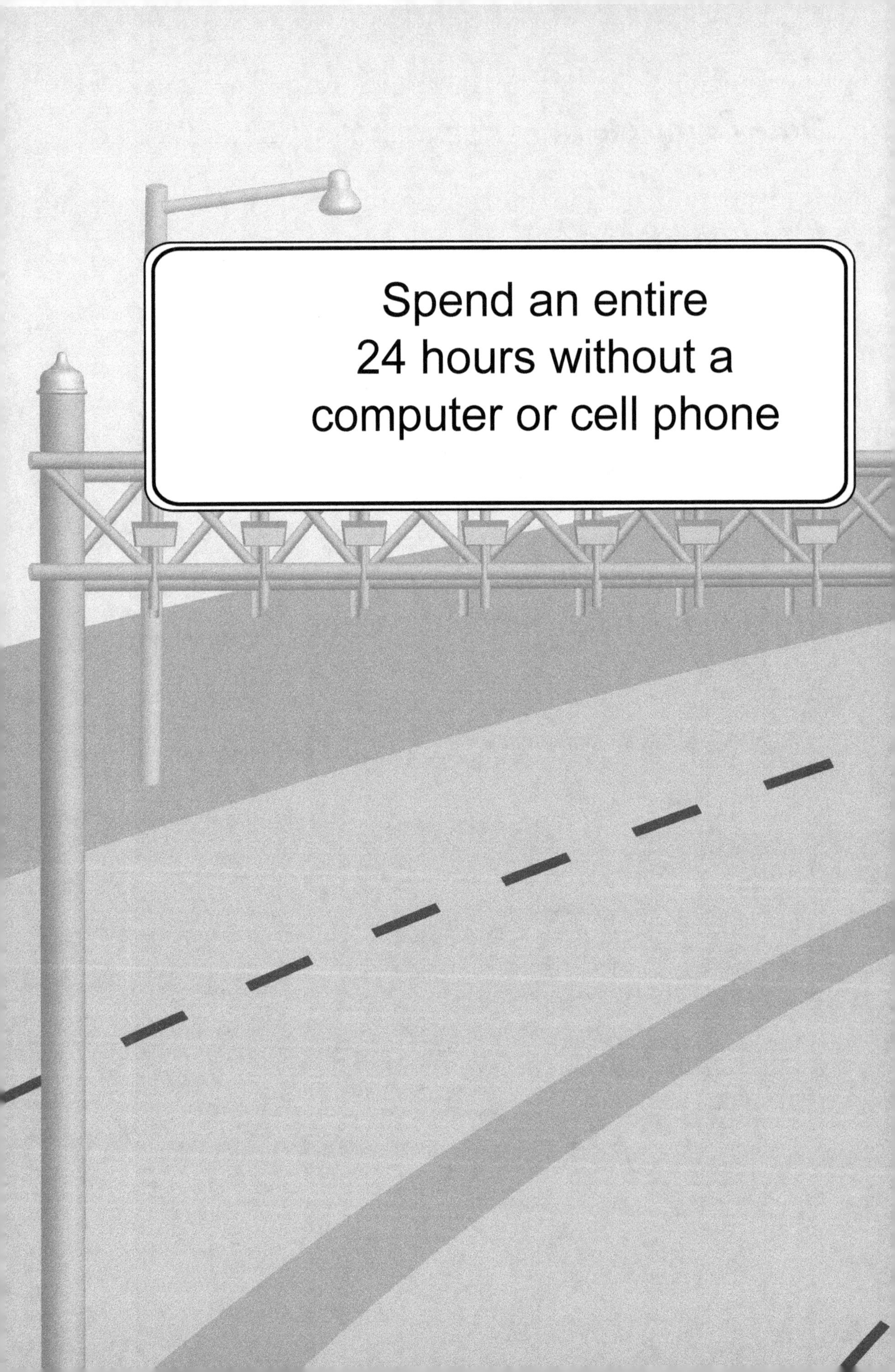

Spend an entire
24 hours without a
computer or cell phone

Date Completed:

What happened?

What did you learn about yourself?

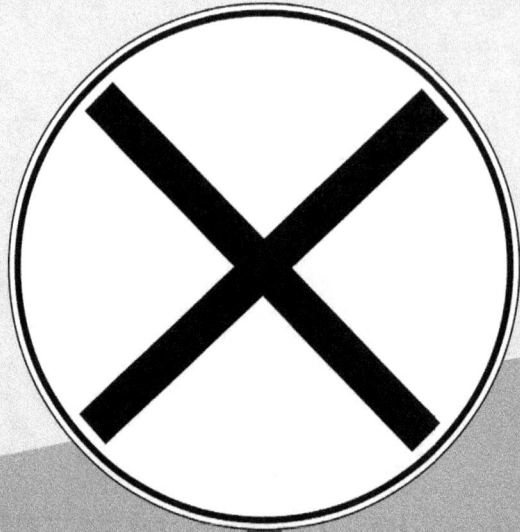

Date Completed: _____

What happened? _____

_____

_____

_____

_____

_____

What did you learn about yourself? _____

_____

_____

_____

_____

_____

_____

_____

_____

_____

Date Completed:

What happened?

What did you learn about yourself?

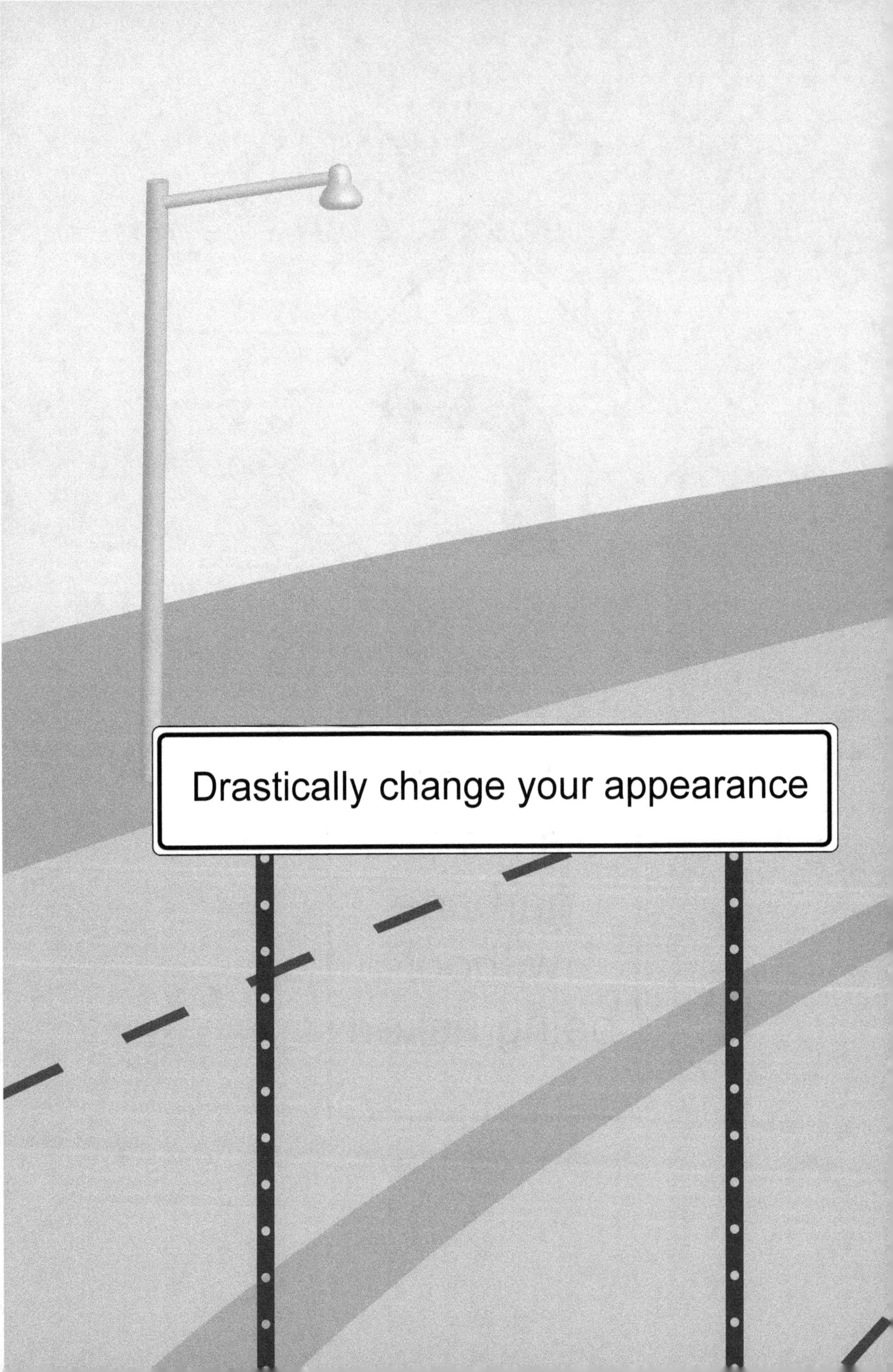
Drastically change your appearance

Date Completed:

What happened?

What did you learn about yourself?

Go
48 hours
without
watching TV or
playing a gaming
system

Date Completed:

What happened?

What did you learn about yourself?

Date Completed:

What happened?

What did you learn about yourself?

Join a club or team

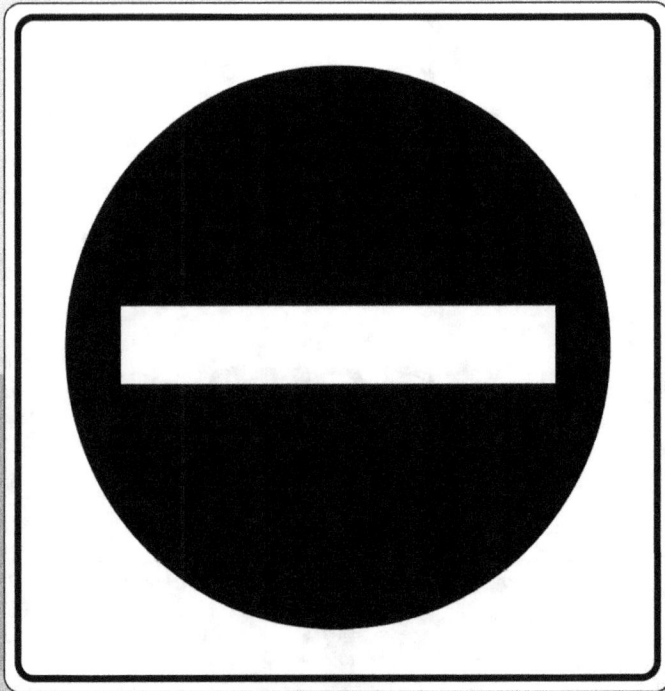

Go to a drop
in centre/
youth centre

Date Completed: _____

What happened?
_____
_____
_____
_____
_____
_____
_____

What did you learn about yourself?
_____
_____
_____
_____
_____
_____
_____
_____
_____
_____
_____

Volunteer

a day for
a
non-profit

Date Completed: _____

What happened?

_____

_____

_____

_____

_____

_____

What did you learn about yourself?

_____

_____

_____

_____

_____

_____

_____

_____

_____

_____

_____

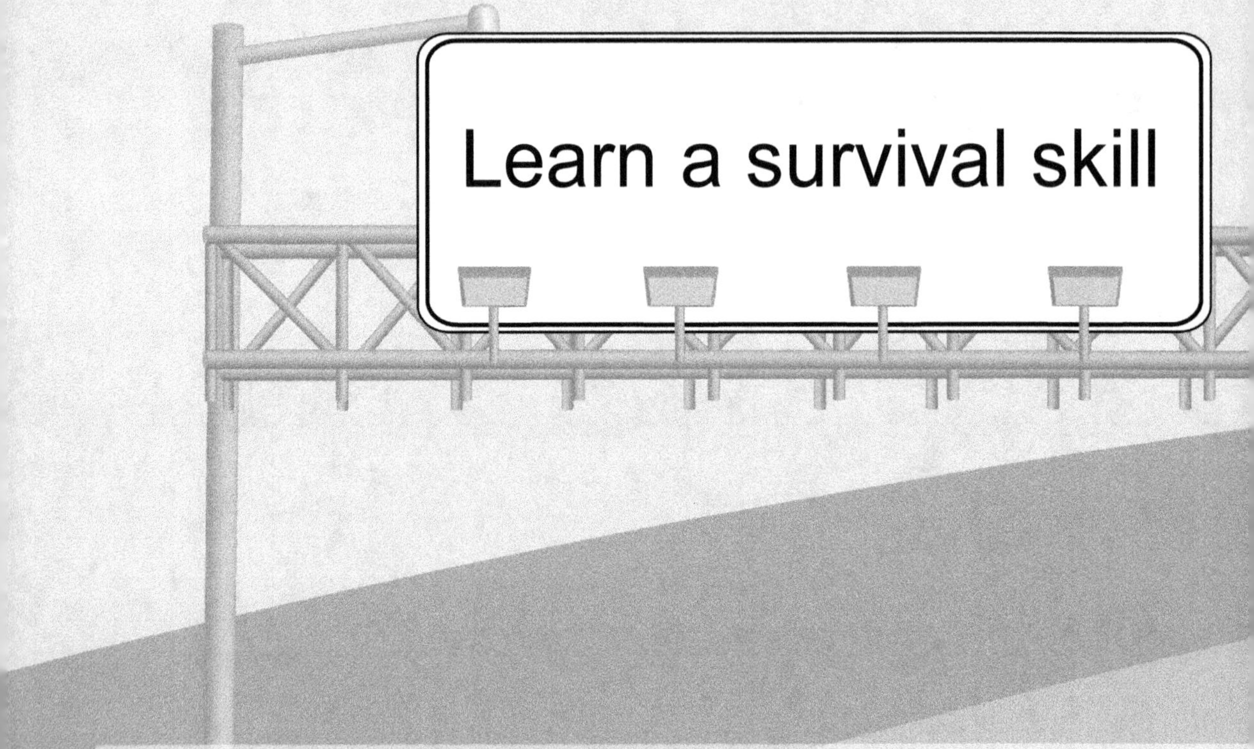
Learn a survival skill

Date Completed: ______________________

____

What happened? ______________________

____

____

____

____

____

____

____

____

What did you learn about yourself?

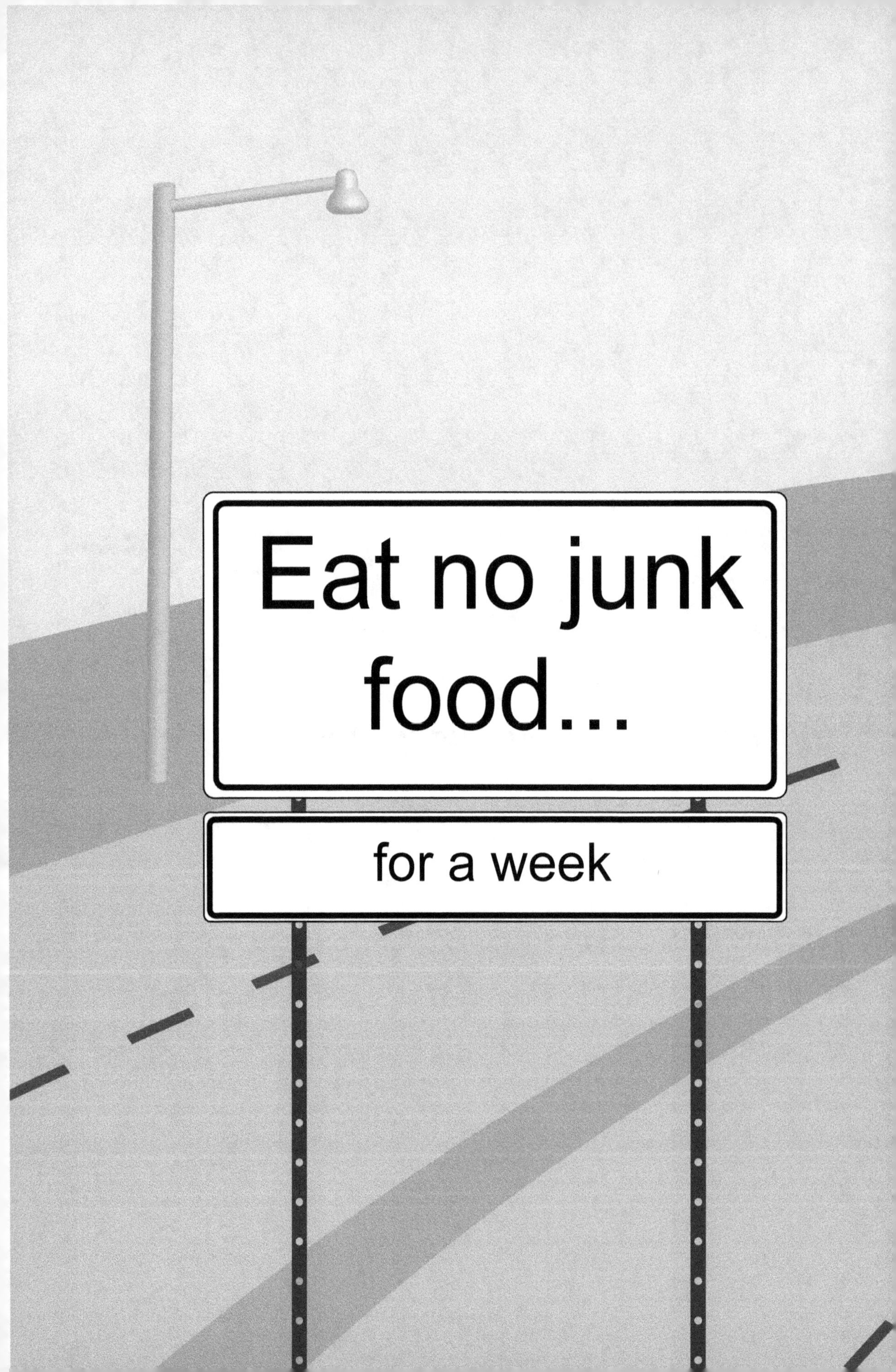
Eat no junk food...
for a week

Date Completed:

What happened?

What did you learn about yourself?

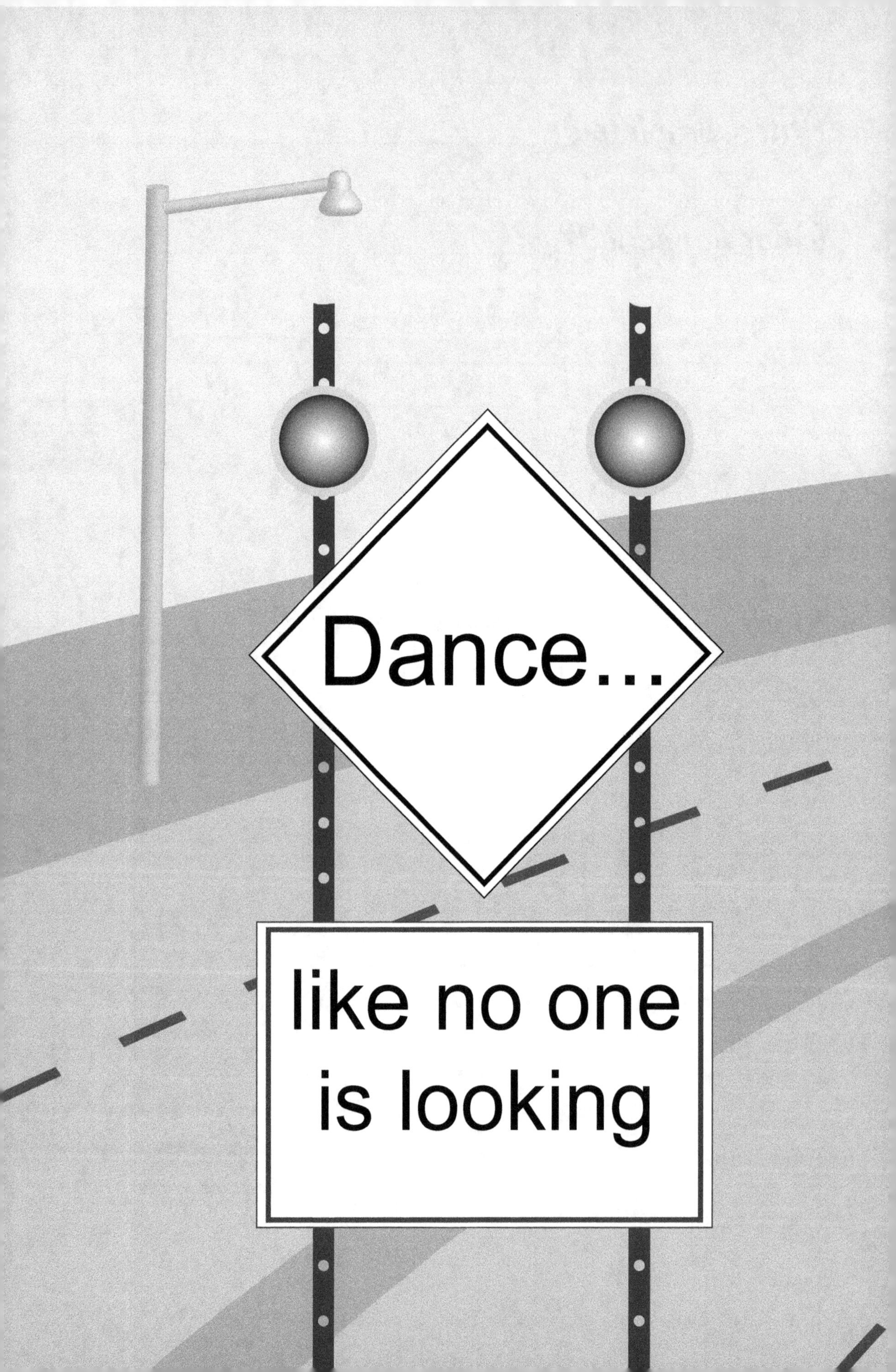
Dance...
like no one
is looking

Date Completed: _____

_____

What happened?

_____

_____

_____

_____

_____

_____

What did you learn about yourself?

_____

_____

_____

_____

_____

_____

_____

_____

_____

_____

_____

Make a speech

Date Completed: _____

What happened?
_____
_____
_____
_____
_____
_____

What did you learn about yourself?
_____
_____
_____
_____
_____
_____
_____
_____
_____
_____

Date Completed: _____

_____

What happened?

_____

_____

_____

_____

_____

_____

What did you learn about yourself?

_____

_____

_____

_____

_____

_____

_____

_____

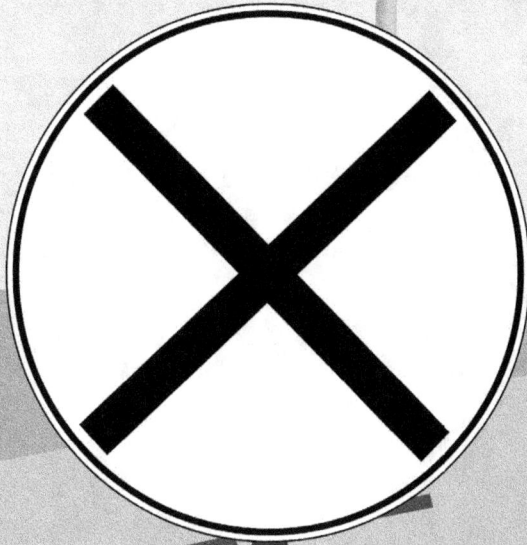

Break a
bad habit

Tell someone

about what is most important to you

Date Completed:

What happened?

What did you learn about yourself?

47

Plant
a tree

Date Completed:

What happened?

What did you learn about yourself?

Date Completed: _____

_____

What happened?

_____

_____

_____

_____

_____

_____

What did you learn about yourself?

_____

_____

_____

_____

_____

_____

_____

_____

Share your lunch
with someone who needs it

End an argument

Date Completed: _____

What happened? _____

_____

_____

_____

_____

_____

_____

_____

_____

What did you learn about yourself?

Date Completed:

What happened?

What did you learn about yourself?

Date Completed: _____

_____

What happened?

_____

_____

_____

_____

_____

What did you learn about yourself?

_____

_____

_____

_____

_____

_____

_____

When you
make a big
mistake...

admit it and apologize

Date Completed: _____

_____

What happened? _____

_____

_____

_____

_____

_____

What did you learn about yourself? _____

_____

_____

_____

_____

_____

_____

_____

_____

_____

_____

Date Completed: _____

What happened? _____

_____

_____

_____

_____

_____

What did you learn about yourself?

_____

_____

_____

_____

_____

_____

_____

_____

_____

Open
a door for someone

Date Completed:

What happened?

What did you learn about yourself?

53
Help
a
Neighbour

Date Completed:

What happened?

What did you learn about yourself?

Date Completed:

What happened?

What did you learn about yourself?

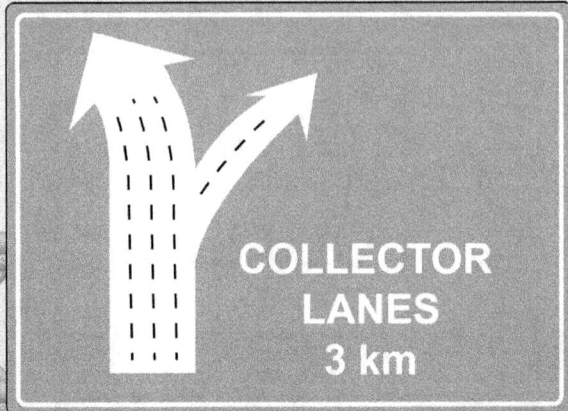

Date Completed:

_____

What happened?

_____

_____

_____

_____

_____

_____

What did you learn about yourself?

_____

_____

_____

_____

_____

_____

_____

_____

_____

_____

Tell someone the
thing that you
like least about
yourself

Date Completed:

What happened?

What did you learn about yourself?

Date Completed:

What happened?

What did you learn about yourself?

5 Replace the toilet paper

Date Completed:

What happened?

What did you learn about yourself?

Date Completed: _____

_____

What happened?

_____

_____

_____

_____

_____

_____

What did you learn about yourself?

_____

_____

_____

_____

_____

_____

_____

_____

Date Completed:

What happened?

What did you learn about yourself?

Date Completed:

What happened?

What did you learn about yourself?

Read
the entire
newspaper

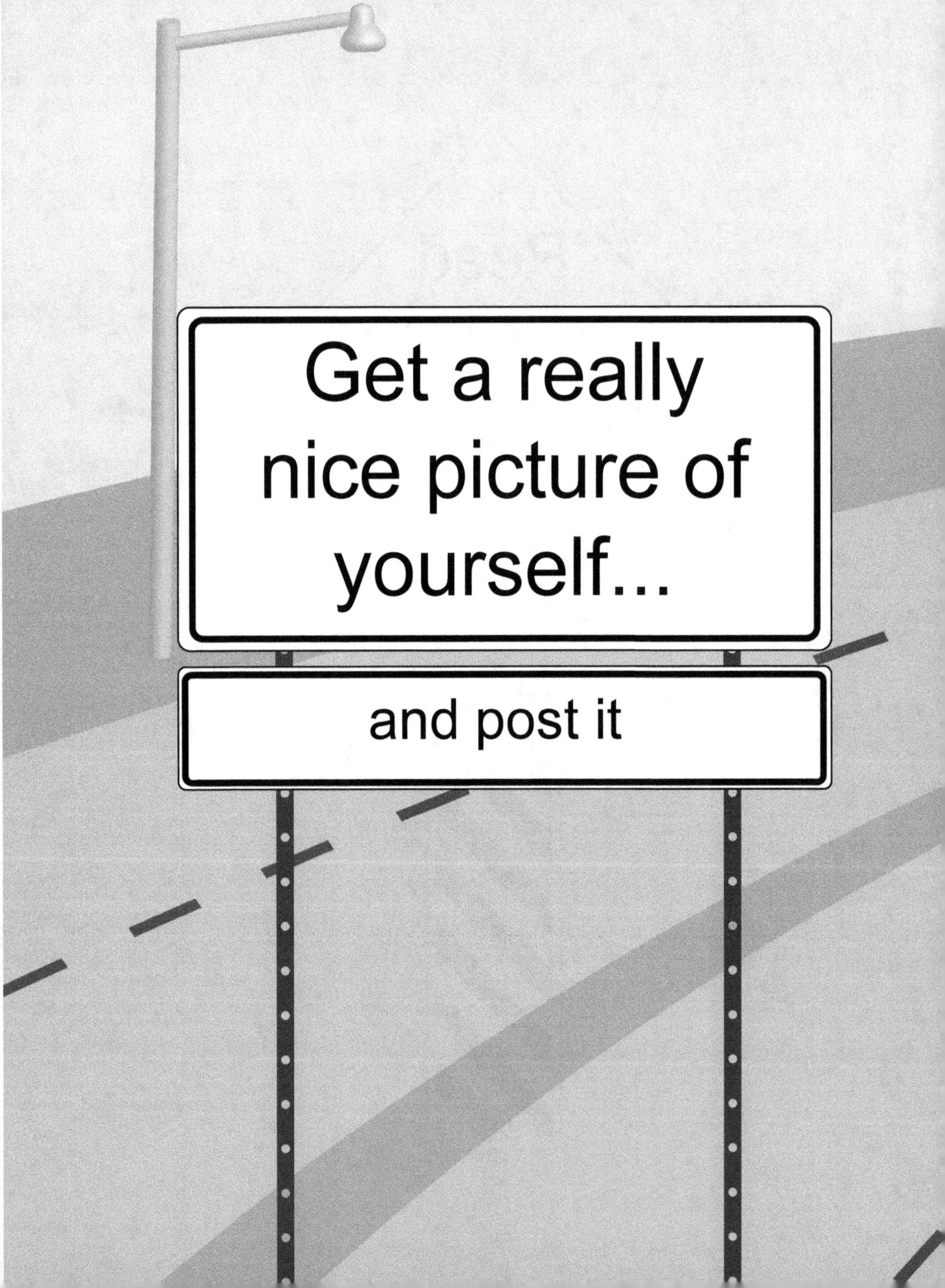
Get a really nice picture of yourself...
and post it

Date Completed: _____

What happened?

_____

_____

_____

_____

_____

_____

What did you learn about yourself?

_____

_____

_____

_____

_____

_____

_____

_____

_____

_____

_____

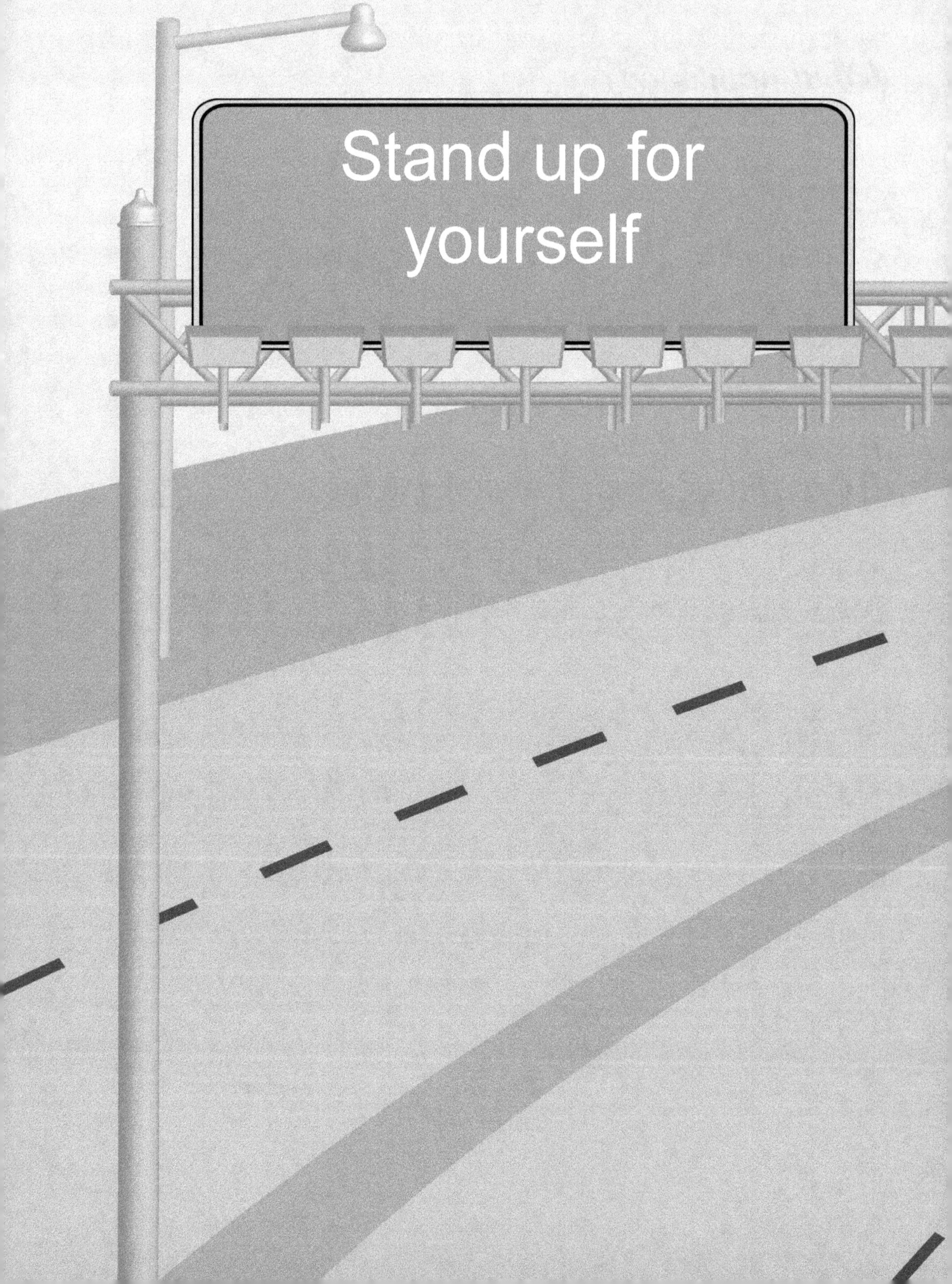
Stand up for
yourself

Date Completed:

What happened?

What did you learn about yourself?

Let go of a bad memory

Date Completed:

_____

What happened?

_____

_____

_____

_____

_____

_____

What did you learn about yourself?

_____

_____

_____

_____

_____

_____

_____

_____

_____

Date Completed: _____

_____

What happened? _____

_____

_____

_____

_____

_____

_____

What did you learn about yourself?

_____

_____

_____

_____

_____

_____

_____

_____

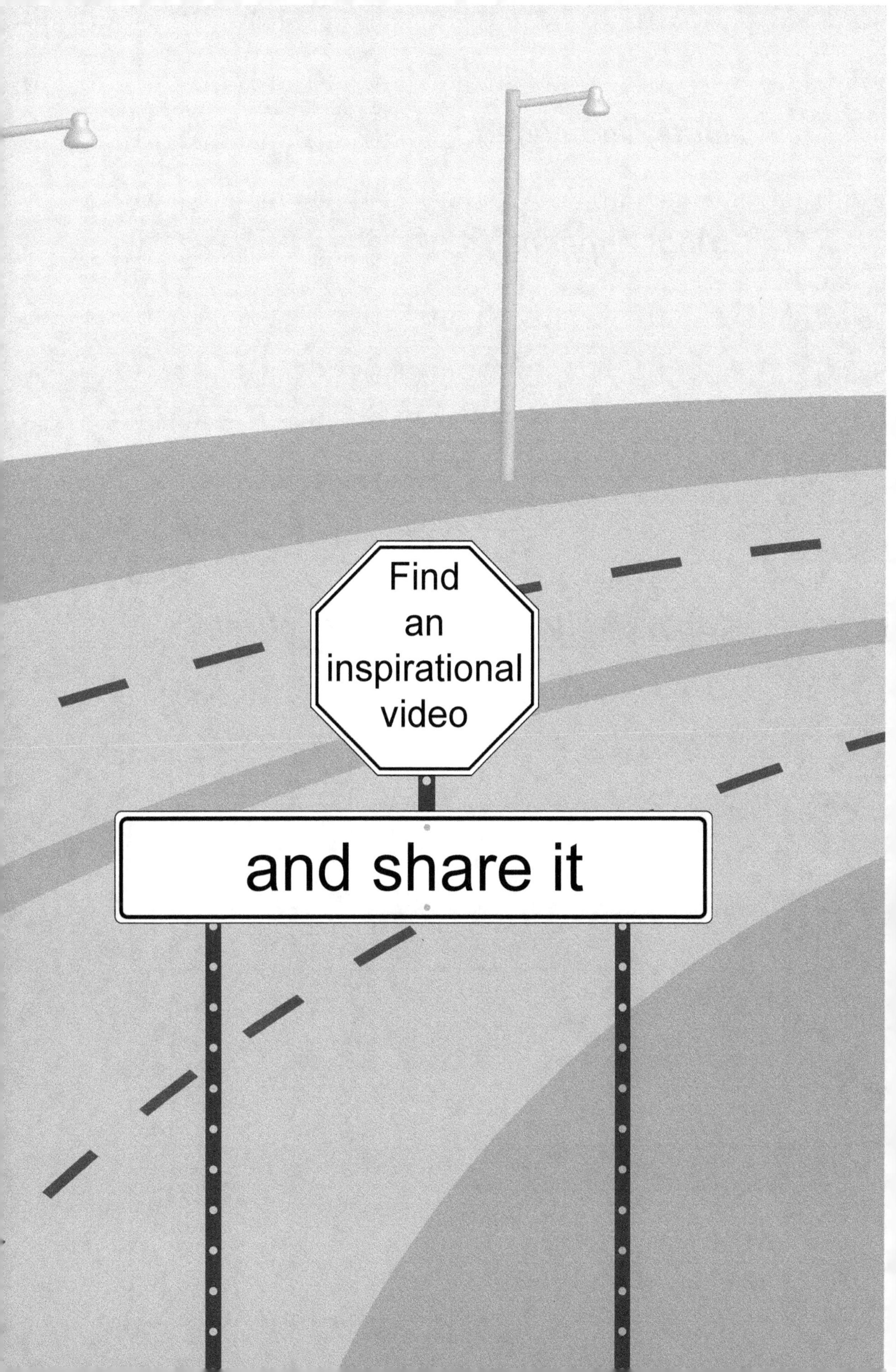
Find
an
inspirational
video
and share it

Date Completed: _____

_____

What happened?
_____
_____
_____
_____
_____
_____
_____

What did you learn about yourself?
_____
_____
_____
_____
_____
_____
_____
_____

Carry someone's packages or groceries to their car

Date Completed: _____

What happened? _____

_____

_____

_____

_____

_____

_____

What did you learn about yourself? _____

_____

_____

_____

_____

_____

_____

_____

_____

Record all of your challenge experiences

Date Completed:

What happened?

What did you learn about yourself?

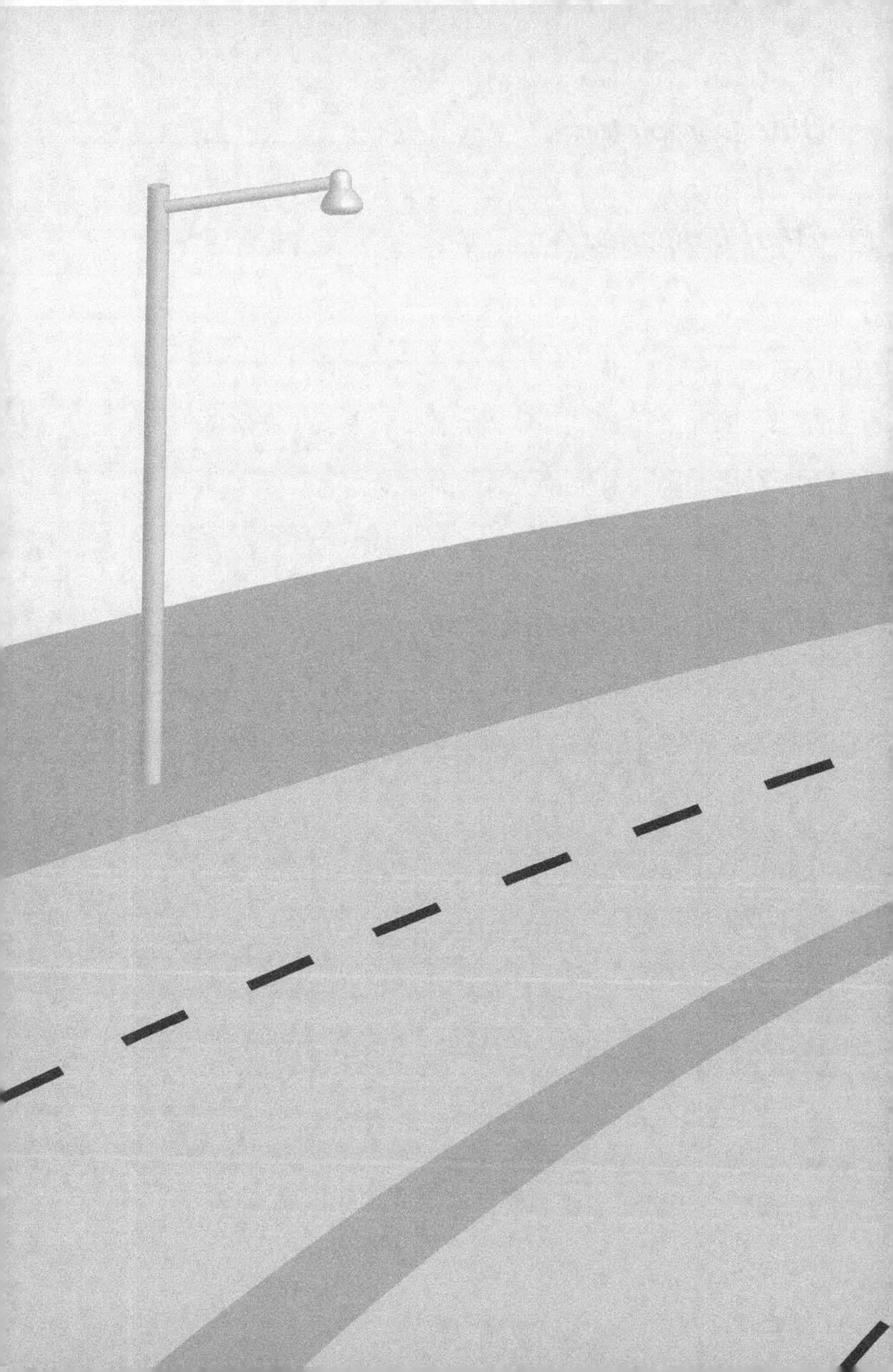

Date Completed:

What happened?

What did you learn about yourself?

www.ingramcontent.com/pod-product-compliance
Lightning Source LLC
LaVergne TN
LVHW081353060426
835510LV00013B/1792